chool

Light and dark

Peter Riley and Dr Brian Knapp

Curriculum Visions

Science@School

Teacher's Guide
There is a Teacher's Guide available to accompany this book.

Dedicated Web Site
There is a wealth of supporting material including videos and activities available at the Professional Zone, part of our dedicated web site:

www.CurriculumVisions.com

The Professional Zone
is a subscription zone.

A CVP Book.
First published in 2008

Copyright © 2008 Earthscape

The rights of Peter Riley and Brian Knapp to be identified as the authors of this work have been asserted by them in accordance with the Copyright, Designs and Patents Act 1988.

Authors
Peter Riley, BSc, C Biol, MI Biol, PGCE, and Brian Knapp, BSc, PhD

Senior Designer
Adele Humphries, BA, PGCE

Educational Consultant
Jan Smith (former Deputy Head of Wellfield School, Burnley, Lancashire)

Editor
Gillian Gatehouse

Designed and produced by
EARTHSCAPE

Printed in China by
WKT Co., Ltd

Curriculum Visions Science@School
Volume 1D Light and dark
A CIP record for this book is available from the British Library.

ISBN: 978 1 86214 256 5

Picture credits
All pictures are from the Earthscape and ShutterStock collections.

This product is manufactured from sustainable managed forests. For every tree cut down at least one more is planted.

You can see yourself in a mirror.

Contents

Weblink: www.curriculumvisions.com

Light and dark

We need light to see.

When there is light we can see the shape of things. We can see their colours.

When it is dark we cannot easily see the shape of things or see their colours.

These canoes are in bright sunlight. You can see their shapes and colours very well.

Here are the same canoes by moonlight. They seem to have no colour, and it is hard to see their shapes.

Weblink: www.curriculumvisions.com

In the day we can
see each tree clearly.

When it is dark we cannot see the trees.

What is it like to see by moonlight?

Sources of light

Many things give out light.

The Sun is the brightest light in our world. It is so bright we cannot look at it.

Most lights are much less bright and we only use them at night.

Here is the Sun shining from a clear blue sky.

Caution: never look directly at the Sun.

Weblink: www.curriculumvisions.com

Neon lights are used for signs.

Car dashboard
lights are quite dim.

Car headlights
shine ahead only.

Power button lights show when
something is switched on.

You may need lots of light bulbs to light a room.

How many light bulbs have you got in your home?

Weblink: www.curriculumvisions.com

Light and burning

When things burn they give out light.

When something burns it gives out light. Candles, fires and fireworks all give out light.

Sparklers give a magical light.

A fireworks' display can light up the ground.

Weblink: www.curriculumvisions.com

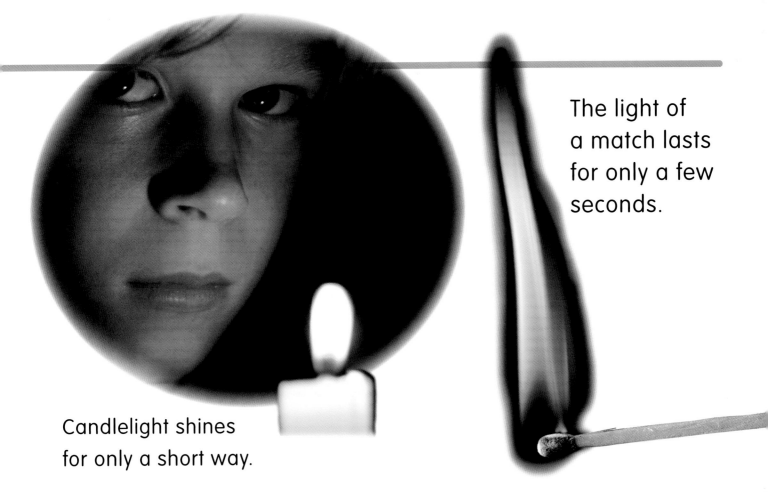

The light of a match lasts for only a few seconds.

Candlelight shines for only a short way.

A wood fire gives out a bright glow.

When do people light candles, fireworks and bonfires?

Weblink: www.curriculumvisions.com

Dim and bright

When there is not much light, it is dim.

Another word for dim is dull.

It is often dull on a cloudy day, or in the woods.

It is dim indoors without the lights on.

It is often dull on a snowy day.

It is often dull on a cloudy day.

It is often dull on a foggy day.

It is sunny in these woods.   It is dim in these woods.

When is the light dim in the sky?

Weblink: www.curriculumvisions.com

Dawn and dusk

Dawn and dusk are at the ends of the day.

Dawn is the time of day when it starts to get light.

Dawn is just before sunrise.

The dawn sky often has pale colours.

Dusk is the time of day when it starts to get dark.

Dusk is just after sunset.

The light gets less and less at dusk.

1 Late afternoon

2 Sunset

How the light changes as the Sun sets.

Weblink: www.curriculumvisions.com

At dawn the sky is dark blue above, and pink on the horizon.

3 Early dusk   **4** Late dusk

Is dusk in the morning or the evening?

Light and shapes

When something is between us and the light we can only see its shape.

If you look towards a bright light, the things in front appear as black shapes. These are called silhouettes.

Here are some people waiting in an airport. You can see them only by their shapes.

Weblink: www.curriculumvisions.com

Here are some shapes. What are they?

Weblink: www.curriculumvisions.com

Shiny objects

Some objects are shiny and show bright areas.

Some things have smooth, shiny surfaces.

Other words we use for shiny are sparkling, gleaming, glossy, polished, glistening, pearl and satin.

You cannot see your face in a shiny object. If you could, it would be a mirror (see page 18).

These boots have been polished. Light bounces from them, making them shine.

This wrapping paper and ribbon are shiny.
The light glistens from them.

Many metals
shine – like
the gold in this
treasure chest.

Pearls are shiny, but
you cannot see your
face in them.

How many shiny objects have you got in your home?

Weblink: www.curriculumvisions.com

Mirrors

You can see things in a mirror.

A mirror is very, very smooth.

Most mirrors are flat pieces of glass.

Some mirrors are made of metal.

A spoon can be a mirror. Even a flat water surface can be a mirror.

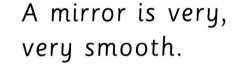

You can see your face in a spoon.

reflection

Weblink: www.curriculumvisions.com

You can see yourself in a lake.

The picture you see in a mirror is called a reflection.

reflection

Cars have mirrors to see the road behind.

reflection

What do you see when you look at yourself in a spoon?

Weblink: www.curriculumvisions.com

9 Keeping safe

We use lights and reflectors to keep safe.

Traffic lights help to keep cars safe.

Lights on cars show where the car is at night.

Reflecting safety strips on our clothes show up in car beams.

Cars use headlights so they can see the road ahead.

People wear shiny reflective strips so they can be seen in the dark.

Weblink: www.curriculumvisions.com

Cars and bikes have reflectors at the back so they can be seen when car headlights shine on them.

Traffic lights tell the cars when to stop or to move safely.

Where are the reflective strips on your coat?

Weblink: www.curriculumvisions.com

Words to learn

Canoe

A small boat with a point at each end.

Horizon

The place far away where the land or sea meets the sky.

horizon

Moonlight

Light shining from the Moon.

Neon lights

Glass tubes which glow with colours when they are switched on.

OPEN
24 HOURS

Reflection

The picture you see in a mirror or in water.

reflection

Reflector

Something that bounces light back. Reflectors are used on the back of bicycles and cars.

Silhouette

The black shape of something. You see it when there is light on the other side of it.

Sunlight

Very strong light from the Sun. Never look directly at the Sun. It can harm your eyes.

Index